DATE DUE		

the
t of
ded
cult
p so
lend
n.

d to

shi)
He
top
d in
nchi
, all

NO NEED FOR TENCHI!

Volume 8: Chef of Iron
VIZ Media Edition

STORY AND ART BY HITOSHI OKUDA

English Adaptation/Fred Burke
Translation/Shuko Shikata
Transcription for Reformat Edition/Alison King
Touch-up Art & Lettering/Bench Press Studios
Design/Courtney Utt
Editor/Shaenon K. Garrity

Managing Editor/Annette Roman
Editorial Director/Elizabeth Kawasaki
Editor in Chief/Alvin Lu
Sr. Director of Acquisitions/Rika Inouye
Sr. VP of Marketing/Liza Coppola
Executive VP of Sales & Marketing/John Easum
Publisher/Hyoe Narita

Printed in the U.S.A.

Published by VIZ Media, LLC
P.O. Box 77010
San Francisco, CA 94107

10 9 8 7 6 5 4 3 2 1
First printing, August 2006

www.viz.com
store.viz.com

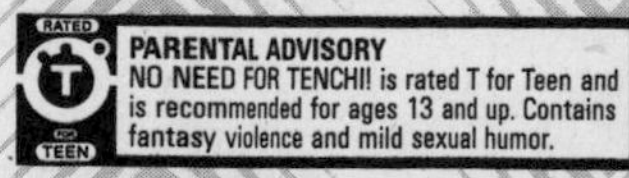

VIZ MANGA

No Need for Tenchi!™

Volume 8: Chef of Iron

STORY AND ART BY

HITOSHI OKUDA

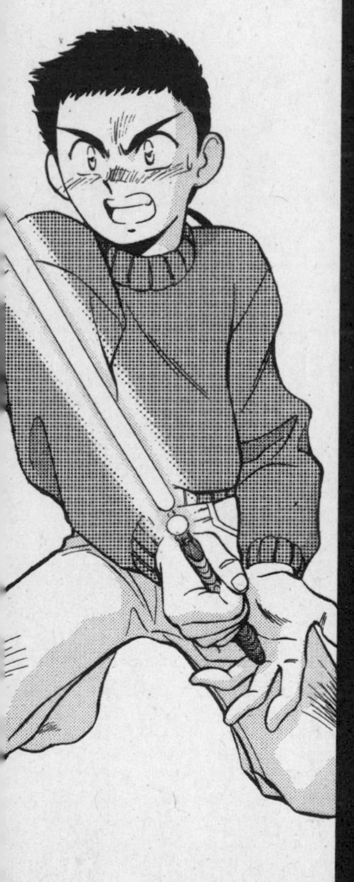

CONTENTS

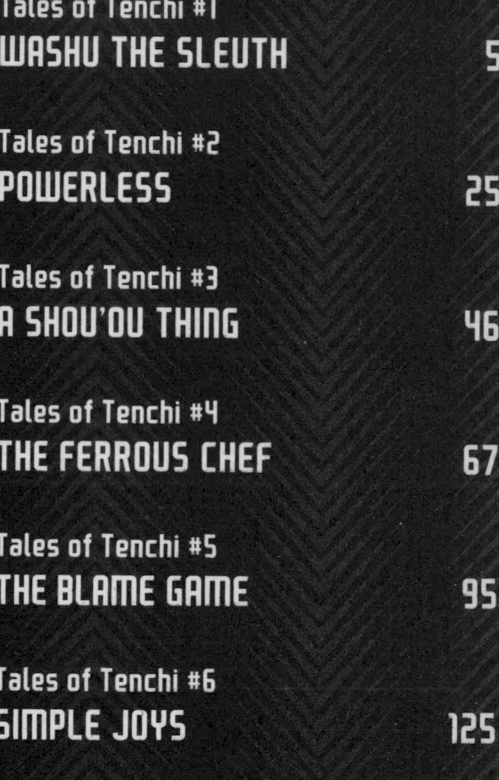

Tales of Tenchi #1:
WASHU THE SLEUTH

THEN WE'LL JUST ASK TENCHI...
ALL RIGHT, EVERYONE-- ACT NORMALLY.
YEP! ♡
OKAY!

YAAAAAAWN...
SOMETIMES MY RESEARCH IS TOO FASCINATING TO *SLEEP*.
HMM?
MORNING, LORD TENCHI. ♡
URK

URK
WHAT'S WITH THE "URK"?
-poke!
UH-OH!
DON'T POKE THE SOUND EFFECTS!

OH! JUST REMEMBERED! LOTS OF ERRANDS TO RUN!
BUT...
...I JUST GOT HERE!

Bianca

SEE YOU LATER, WASHU!
WELL, HE'S SURE TWITCHY TODAY.
...
VROOM!

SEE YOU LATER. BE CAREFUL OF TRAFFIC, TENCHI.
I'M OFF, THEN, SASAMI.
NOT THE SORT OF MAGAZINES I'D EXPECT FOR LORD TENCHI...
OOOH!
ANOTHER SUBJECT FOR INVESTIGATION! ♡

WELL, NOTHING TERRIBLY UNEXPECTED *THUS* FAR.
LOOKS LIKE HE'S GOING TO TOWN.

...AND HE'S NOT IN TOWN YET!
fssh
IT *HAS* BEEN A WHILE SINCE I ATE...
GRMMM
SASAAAMI! ♡
QUK
W-WASHU! YOU FORGOT BREAKFAST, DIDN'T YOU? I'LL WHIP UP AN EARLY LUNCH...JUST A SEC...
SORRY FOR THE TROUBLE.
HOW ABOUT SOME RICE BALLS, WHILE YOU'RE AT IT?
I'M AT A DELICATE POINT IN MY RESEARCH, YOU KNOW...
HERE YOU GO! I THOUGHT RICE BALLS *ALONE* MIGHT BE TOO SIMPLE, SO THERE'S MISO SOUP AND SOME GREENS.
WOW, THANKS A LOT! ♡

BY THE WAY...
HMM?

WAS LORD TENCHI ACTING *ODDLY* THIS MORNING?
URK
URK

O-ODDLY? I DON'T KNOW.
OKAY.

BREEP! BREEP!

GOTTA RUN!
THANKS FOR THE LUNCH. ♡
HA HA HA! NO PROBLEM!

WASHU IS SO PERCEPTIVE.

SHE'S A GENIUS, ALL RIGHT.

MREOW!!

OOH, RIGHT ON TIME! GOOD CAMERA POSITION, TOO. ♡

BA-BOOP!

NOW, LORD TENCHI... WHAT ARE YOU UP TO? ♡

breep!

PWEEP

HMM?

ER... UM...

PLEASE! GET RID OF HIM!

SO THIS *LAME* GUY'S YOUR TYPE?

WHEN YOU COULD HAVE *ME?*

PLEASE GET HIM OFF ME, MISTER!

HE WON'T LEAVE ME ALONE!

WHAT AN OBNOXIOUS DISPLAY.

LORD TENCHI HAS NO LUCK.

COME HERE!

FWAK

....

SORRY.
REFLEX...
OW... OWW!
SHWP

I'LL GET YOU FOR THIS!
FWISH!
UM, ARE YOU OKAY?

WHY'D YOU PICK SOME KINDA MARTIAL ARTS DUDE?
HEY, YOU ALL RIGHT?
DARN IT! OW, OW, OW!

HEY! THE GIRL IS GONE, TOO...
BUT WE'VE NEVER EVEN MET BEF--

A GOOD HAUL, I'LL GIVE YOU THAT!

HE'S *FLOATIN'* IN DOUGH, THAT LITTLE JERK. ♡

COOL! LET'S GO BUY A VIDEO GAME!

A GOOD ONE'S COMING OUT TODAY. ♡

A SCIENTIST'S WORK IS NEVER DONE!

URK

WH-- WHO'S THERE?

I'M SURE GLAD I WAS ON THE CASE TODAY!

HOW *DARE* YOU MISCREANTS ABUSE LORD TENCHI'S SWEET NATURE?

WHAT'S THIS LI'L TOY?

MUST BE HANGIN' BY A WIRE OR SOME-THIN'.

KABOOM!
WHAT WAS THAT? A GAS EX- PLOSION?

PLONK!
!?

MY WALLET ...
HUH?

I SWEAR, LORD TENCHI GIVES ME SO MUCH TROUBLE.
crnch mnch

BUT THAT'S WHAT'S SO CUTE ABOUT HIM. ♡
HA HA... AHA HA HA...
WHAT THE HECK WAS THAT?
Vending
Candy Shop

HE DEFINITELY DOESN'T WANT TO BE SEEN...
BEEPA!
DOOP!
BOOP!

COULD HE *BE* ANY MORE CON-SPICUOUS?

FWIP
FWIP

A GIFT? IS THERE A BIRTHDAY COMING UP?
BREDOOP
NO!
NOT IN THE DATA-BASE!

IT WOULD BE EASIER TO JUST ASK LORD TENCHI...
...BUT HE'S TRYING SO HARD TO KEEP IT A SECRET!

AWWWW...I SHOULDN'T INTERFERE WITH SUCH A SWEET PLAN...

RIGHT, LORD TENCHI?

HEH...

JUST KIDDING!!!

HEH HEH!

GENIUS

HEH HEH!

HEH HEH!

BESIDES, MY PRIDE AS A GENIUS WOULD NEVER LET ME TAKE THE EASY WAY OUT!

!!

WAIT! C-COULD IT BE...

...THAT LORD TENCHI LIKES TO CROSS-DRESS?

THANK YOU!
HUH?
HE BOUGHT IT ALREADY?

DARN IT...
IF I'D CAUGHT THE *SIZE* OF THE CLOTHES, I COULD'VE NARROWED DOWN THE POSSIBILITIES.

!
FWSSSH
I KNOW!

BWAM!!

THIS COULD BE A TEST THAT GOD HAS GIVEN TO THE GREAT-EST GENIUS OF THE UNIVERSE!

FINE! I'LL SOLVE THIS MYSTERY...AND I'LL SOLVE IT BY DINNER TIME!

JUST YOU WATCH!
WASHU! DINNER'S READY!
ARGH! T-TIME'S UP...
glah
HOW COULD SUCH A PRIMITIVE MYSTERY ELUDE MY GREAT INTELLECT?
gleh
PWOP!
PWOP!
PWOP!
!!

WASHU!
HAPPY BIRTH DAY! ♡

HERE'S YOUR PRESENT. ♡
EVERYONE CHIPPED IN, AND I PICKED IT OUT.
I HOPE YOU LIKE IT.
HOW DOES IT LOOK?
WOW, YOU LOOK SO PRETTY, WASHU. ♡
AND LORD TENCHI DID A GREAT JOB! IT'S WONDERFUL! ♡
? !
TODAY'S NOT MY BIRTHDAY.
HUH?

YOU'RE SO CLUE-LESS!
THE IDEA IS TO FOOL PEOPLE ON APRIL FOOL'S DAY!
GOTCHA! ♪
OH, THAT! APRIL FOOL'S!
DO WE EVER HAVE A FEAST TONIGHT! ♡
OOH. ♡
FSSSHT
AND YELLING LIKE THAT IS RUDE!
...
WHAT DID YOU SAY? LOOK WHO'S TALKING!
WEREN'T YOU THE ONE WHO SAID TODAY WAS WASHU'S BIRTHDAY?
RYOKO !!
TEE HEE
NOW...
NOW...
FIRST OF ALL...

WITH THIS FABULOUS MEAL TO EAT, WHO CARES? SASAMI WENT TO ALL THIS TROUBLE...
I THINK I'M STARTING TO UNDERSTAND...
...SO THE LEAST WE CAN DO IS ENJOY IT! ♡
...THAT A FEW THINGS IN LIFE ARE MORE FUN WHEN THEY'RE UNPREDICTABLE. ♡
HAPPY BIRTHDAY AGAIN, WASHU!
POP
HAPPY BIRTHDAY!
PWOP!
OH, DEAR!
WE'RE SHORT BY 19,000 CANDLES.
SORRY!
I'M GOING TO *HIT* YOU!
HAPPY 20,000TH BIRTHDAY!

Tales of Tenchi #2:
POWERLESS

WASHU CAN READ RYOKO'S THOUGHTS WHILE THEY ARE CONNECTED BY THE ASTRAL RING.

I DON'T KNOW WHY YOU THINK THIS TAPE IS SO EMBARRASSING. ♡
DON'T LEAVE ME BEHIND! DON'T LEAVE ME ALONE!
YOU'RE SO CUTE, RYOKO. ♡
TURN THAT DARN THING OFF!

▲SEE OAV EP. 13

ENOUGH FUN. LET'S START WITH A *POTENTIAL* CHECK. ♪

HMM...WITH ONLY ONE JEWEL, THE ENTROPY LIMIT VALUE IS LOW AFTER ALL.
BEEP!
BOOP!

NOW, WHERE DID I PUT RYOKO'S PERSONAL DATA FILE?
?
ULGUP!

ISN'T THAT IT BY YOUR FEET? GETTIN' SENILE! ♪

YOU'RE SO RUDE, RYOKO.

SHLIKT
LORD TENCHI WOULD NOT FIND THAT ATTRACTIVE!

A SLICE...CUT OUT OF SPACE?
WASHU, JUMP TO YOUR RIGHT!

SKLIST
WHOA !!

YOW!
ZZTT
ZZTT
ZLSS SHT

SSZZZTTT
ZZLLT
ZZTTT
ZSHTTT

WOW!
ka-BWAM
NOT ONLY CAN YOU *TRANSFORM*, BUT YOU CAN *TELEPORT*, TOO. ♪
YOU'RE AN IMPORTANT SAMPLE! I'M *NOT* GOING TO LET YOU *ESCAPE!*
SKRAK
FWISH FWISH
FWOOMSH
SHWAAAAAAA

SHSHT

SHEESH! WHAT A *PAIN* YOU ARE!

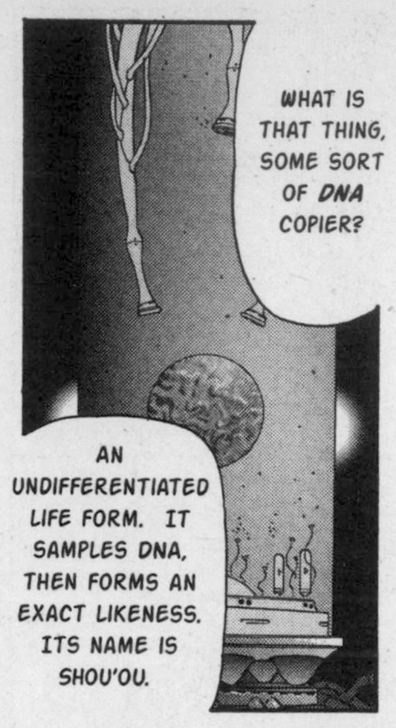

WHAT IS THAT THING, SOME SORT OF *DNA* COPIER?
AN UNDIFFERENTIATED LIFE FORM. IT SAMPLES DNA, THEN FORMS AN EXACT LIKENESS. ITS NAME IS SHOU'OU.

YOU KNOW OF BIO-MIMICRY, DON'T YOU?
OF COURSE.
THAT'S WHEN AN ANIMAL PROTECTS ITSELF BY TAKING ON THE SHAPE OR COLOR OF ANOTHER ANIMAL, PLANT, OR OBJECT, RIGHT?

YEAH, THERE ARE TWO TYPES: *CRYPTIC COLORATION*, OR CAMOUFLAGE, WHICH MATCHES THE SURROUNDINGS...AND BATESIAN MIMICRY, WHICH COPIES AN ANIMAL WITH *APOSEMATIC COLORATION.*
BOTH SERVE AS PROTECTION FROM PREDATORS.
THEN THIS GUY, TOO?

SOUTHEASTERN ASIA'S CAMOUFLAGED LEAF INSECT

NO, SHOU'OU IS A LITTLE MORE AGGRESSIVE THAN THAT.
IT TRANSFORMS TO THROW ITS PREY OFF GUARD.

WHY GO TO ALL THE TROUBLE?
WHY NOT JUST TELEPORT?
TELEPORTATION APPEARS TO USE UP AN INORDINATE AMOUNT OF ENERGY.
IT'S A METHOD OF LAST RESORT.
THIS TIME I PUT AN ANTI-TELEPORTATION DEVICE ON ITS CAGE, SO WE *SHOULD* BE OKAY.

ANYWAY, WE'RE DONE FOR TODAY, RIGHT?
I'M GOING TO *EAT*.
TELL SASAMI THAT I'LL BE RIGHT THERE.
!
...
!?
WHAT'S THE MATTER, RYOKO?

THAT ANTI-TELE-PORT LOCK!
DID YOU PUT ONE IN *THIS* ROOM TOO?
?
NO, I HAVEN'T.

I...
I CAN'T TELE-PORT...
vreep
WHAT?

I'M NOT LUCKY AT ALL, DAMMIT...
SNARF SNARF
IT WAS BAD TIMING.
THE DEVICE BROKE JUST AS WE WERE ON AN ABILITIES CROSS-CHECK.
SECONDS, PLEASE! ♡
BUT YOU'RE LUCKY IT DOESN'T AFFECT DAY-TO-DAY LIFE!
WHEN ARE YOU GOING TO GET ME BACK TO NORMAL?
LET'S SAY A WEEK. I HAVE TO WORK ON BOTH YOU AND THE DEVICE.
WELL, JUST BE CAREFUL NOT TO HIT YOUR HEAD WHEN YOU TRY TO GO THROUGH WALLS.
tee hee hee
AYEKA...
JERK...
JUST YOU WAIT UNTIL I GET MY POWERS BACK...
SNIKT
I'M STUFFED. ♡
CLINK
TINK
SASAMI, THAT WAS DELISH. THANKS FOR THE MEAL.
HEE HEE! THANKS, TENCHI. ♡
LET'S SEE... TONIGHT'S DISH DUTY IS...

RYOKO.
URK.
I-I'M GOING FOR A LITTLE WALK. ♡
fwshh
OH! RYOKO...
HERE WE GO.
SLAM
SHE'S *ALREADY* FORGOTTEN LADY AYEKA'S WARNING.
UNNNNGGGHH

OH, RYOKO?
COULD YOU WIPE OFF THE GREASE WITH A PAPER TOWEL FIRST?
WHAT? WHY BOTHER?
scrub
IT MAKES IT EASIER IN THE LONG RUN.
FINE, I'LL DO IT, I'LL DO IT...
SLINK

HMM...
...
...
WHY ARE YOU STARING AT ME?
OH, I'M SORRY.
ARE THERE SOAP SUDS ON MY FACE?
NO, THAT'S NOT IT.
I'VE JUST NEVER SEEN YOU DOING DISHES BEFORE!
WHEN I WATCH YOU DOING THE CHORES LIKE THIS...
...WELL, YOU LOOK REALLY *HOMEY,* LIKE A *HOUSE-WIFE!*
HUH?
BADOOM!

YOU MEAN LIKE TENCHI'S MY HUSBAND AND I'M THE W-WIFE! ♡
SAY, DO I REALLY LOOK LIKE A HOUSE-WIFE?
YEAH.
S-SURE.
JUST DON'T FLING THE KNIFE AROUND, PLEASE...

ALL RIGHT, THEN! BRING ME ALL THE DISHES! ♡

AND EVER SINCE...

RYOKO TOOK TO HER CHORES AS IF SHE HAD FOUND A NEW JOY...

HAH!
SKRAK
YAH
KLOP
CHUP
CHOP!
CHUP
...AND THREE DAYS QUICKLY PASSED!
KLOP! CHOP!
ALL RIGHT, THAT'LL DO FOR TODAY.
HFF
TH-THANK YOU, SIR.
UFF
TENCHI, GOOD WORK. ♡
HERE'S YOUR TOWEL.
OH, THANKS.

?
THANKS. ♡

YOU HARDLY EVER COME WATCH MY TRAINING.
WELL, YOU KNOW I CAN'T USE MY POWERS NOW...IT'S MADE ME APPRECIATE THE STUFF I DON'T USUALLY DO.

ahem
I HAVE SOME BUSINESS AT MISS UJIKO'S HOUSE.
OH, GRANDPA.
SEE YOU LATER.

YUM.
THIS IS DELICIOUS.

REALLY?
YOU MEAN IT?
I-I WOULDN'T LIE.
IT'S DELI-CIOUS.

I WON'T MENTION HOW IT *LOOKS*, THOUGH.
AW, YOU'RE SO SWEET!
TEE HEE!
HA HA HA HA HA!

THIS REMINDS ME OF MY MOTHER.
YOUR MOM?

I....LIKED IT HERE. WE USED TO COME HERE AND PLAY.

I USED TO EAT RICE BALLS WITH HER SOMETIMES...
...

I SEE...
...
YOU...
YOU DON'T TALK MUCH ABOUT YOUR MOM.

SHE HAD JURAI BLOOD IN HER, DIDN'T SHE?
I WONDER IF SHE COULD PRODUCE LIGHT HAWK WINGS, LIKE YOU CAN.

WHO KNOWS?

I ONLY HAVE MEMORIES FROM WHEN I WAS LITTLE, BUT SHE NEVER ONCE USED JURAI POWERS...
SHE WASN'T ANY DIFFERENT FROM THE OTHER MOMS.
BUT...
BUT?

I DO KNOW...

...THAT I LOVED HER MORE THAN *ANYONE*.

...

WHAT IS IT?
S- SAY... WASHU...
ALL RIGHT.
UM... WELL...
HOW MUCH LONGER... YOU KNOW, UNTIL IT'S ALL FIXED?
THIS WILL BE ALL FOR TODAY.
DON'T RUSH ME.
I'M DOING MY BEST.
beep boop!
OH, UM... YOU DON'T HAVE TO RUSH.
OH... REALLY ?

HMM?
(MAYBE I CAN STAY THIS WAY A LITTLE LONGER...)
HEY!
OH?

A-ANYWAY, IF YOU'RE GOING TO FIX IT, DO IT RIGHT!
OKAY, OKAY!

KLONK!
TEE HEE! ♡

WHEW, THAT WAS CLOSE.

OH, RYOKO.

AREN'T YOU ON LAUNDRY DUTY TODAY?
OH, WAS I?

!
SORRY, I'LL DO THAT RIGHT AWAY.

AS A SCIENTIST AND A MOTHER, I MUST COLLECT DATA ON ALL ACTION PATTERNS WHICH OCCUR DURING SUCH INTERESTING CIRCUMSTANCES! ♡
heh! heh!
SORRY ABOUT THAT, AYEKA.

TH-THIS REALLY MESSES WITH MY MIND.

STILL, THERE'S REALLY NO REASON TO RUSH THINGS! ♡
ACTUALLY, I SOLVED THE PROBLEM EVEN QUICKER THAN I EXPECTED! RYOKO WILL HAVE HER POWERS BACK JUST AS SOON AS I INJECT THIS MICRO-MACHINE.

WHOA!!

WUFF!

WHFFF

EEEK!

wifff

KA-KRESH

!?

FITT FITT FITT FITT FITT

MI-HOSHI, WHAT THE HECK...
...DO YOU THINK YOU'RE DOING?
OH, SORRY!!
I WAS LOOKING FOR SASAMI, AND THERE WAS THIS COCKROACH, AND...

PWOP!

...EE...

EEEEEEEEK!!
FWUMP!

...
I GUESS THAT'S ONE WAY TO KEEP HER QUIET...

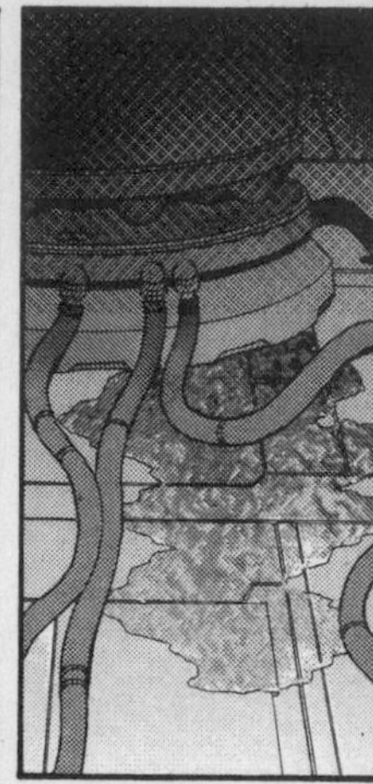

C'MON, MIHOSHI, WAKE UP!

NO USE.
SHE'S OUT COLD.

SHEESH!!

I HOPE SHE DIDN'T BREAK ANYTHING ELSE.

RYOKO.
URK.

Tales of Tenchi #3:
A SHOU'OU THING

HOW DOES LADY MIHOSHI *ALWAYS* MANAGE TO GET THROUGH MY BARRIER FIELD?
I GUESS THAT'S JUST HER GENIUS...
SHWOOP
TWEE
TWEE
SHLOOP
!!

KERSPLISH
HMM! THAT STRANGE FEELING...
kreek!
SASAMI, WHERE ARE YOU OFF TO?
I'VE MADE TENCHI'S LUNCH, AND NOW I'M GOING TO DELIVER IT. ♡
TENCHI? ♡ CAN I GO WITH YOU?
SURE, RYOKO!

SQUIP
SQUOP

THE FEEDING PATTERNS OF WASHU'S NEW LIFE FORM WERE *VERY* PECULIAR.
THE *SHOU'OU* NEITHER KILLS ITS PREY NOR LETS THEM LIVE, BUT GRADUALLY ABSORBS THEIR ENERGY...
UNGH...
BLUP!
ME, THE *GENIUS*...
...MY ENERGY DRAINING AWAY. AWFUL!

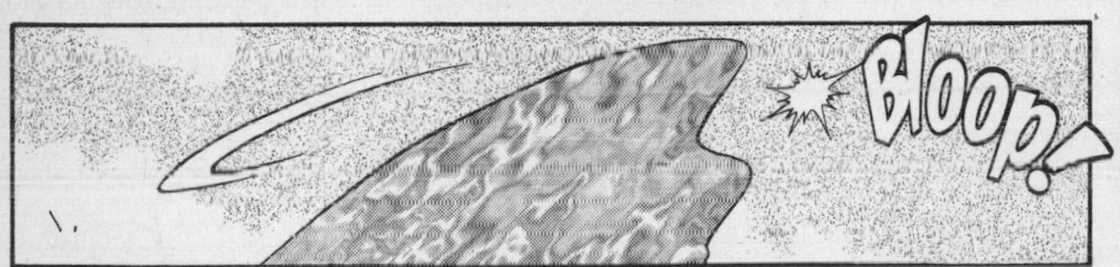
BLOOP!

IT'S SENSING A LARGE ENERGY SOURCE...
WHAT? I WASN'T ENOUGH?

FWASHT
COULD IT BE...

IT'S BEEN SO LONG SINCE WE JUST ***WALKED*** LIKE THIS!

YOU USUALLY FLY OFF BY YOURSELF.

THAT'S TRUE.

SAY...

?

DOES IT BOTHER YOU, NOT HAVING YOUR POWERS?

SURE, IT WAS A REAL PAIN AT FIRST. I EVEN THOUGHT I WOULDN'T BE ABLE TO FIGHT WITH AYEKA!

HA HA... THOUGHT SO!

BUT I'VE ALSO LEARNED SOME THINGS BECAUSE OF THIS.

WHEN I'M WORKING JUST LIKE A NORMAL EARTH-LING...

...IT FEELS LIKE TENCHI IS... ***PLEASED*** SOMEHOW.

TENCHI'S ***MOM*** MUST NOT HAVE USED ANY SPECIAL POWERS WHEN HE WAS GROWING UP...
...

OOPS!

THAT WAS REALLY OUT OF CHARACTER.
DON'T TELL TENCHI OR AYEKA ABOUT THIS.
TEE HEE! I DON'T KNOW! ♡

HEY, SASAMI!
JUST KIDDING! I WON'T TELL!

WHEW!
fssht

SKROP
SKROP

JILP
JILUP

BLOOPA

SPLRRR
MMSH

WHEN'D YOU GET HERE?
HUH?
TENCHI! WASHU! HELLO UP THERE!

OH!

MYOWP!

MYA MREOW!!
I FEEL GREAT ENERGY...
I WANT TO EAT IT TO EAT IT TO EAT EAT EAT EAT!
!?
WASHU, I DIDN'T SEE YOU THERE!
EAT EAT EAT EAT EEEEATTTTT!
I WANT TO EAT IT!
SKLORSH
!!

KEEEEEE
UNGH!
TENCHI!
HIS ENERGY... TOO BIG...
I HATE HIM, I HATE HIM, I HATE HIM!
SKRRK

GONE! TELEPORTED AWAY!

TENCHI!
TENCHI, ARE YOU ALL RIGHT?
YEAH...
BUT THAT WASN'T *WASHU* JUST NOW, WAS IT?

IT'S WASHU'S NEW LIFE FORM... THE *SHOU'OU.*
THE *SHOU'OU* ABSORBS ITS PREY, THEN *IMITATES* IT TO TRICK OTHERS...
!
?

UH-OH!
FSSH
RYOKO!
WHERE ARE YOU GOING?

JUST PROTECT SASAMI!

PRO-TECT HER?
YOU MEAN, FROM THAT THING?
UMM... SAY, TENCHI...

WOULDN'T SHE...
BE IN DANGER, TOO?
OH, NO!
VROOOOOM
RYO-OH-KI! WHERE'D IT GO?
MEOW MYA MEOW!
WHAT?
BELOW?
SPLOOOWSH
SPLIRMSH!

TMP
TMP
TMP
TMP
TMP
TMP
TMP
SKRRK
RMB RMB
RMB
RMB
RMB
THAT'S ...
...NOT RYOKO.
BLOOB
WH...
WHERE AM I?
!
OH! BUT WHERE'S WASHU?

THE *SHAME!* THIS *HYPERSPACE* HAS GOT ME BEAT...

ME! A TOP-FLIGHT GENIUS! BUT...

FWOP

WASHU! AND MIHOSHI, *TOO?*

RYOKO, OVER HERE!

TATOON

...IF I INJECT YOU WITH THIS, YOU'LL GET YOUR POWERS BACK.

BUT YOU'LL NO LONGER BE AN EARTHLING! YOU'LL BE YOUR OLD SELF!

THE WAY I WAS...

TENCHI!

WHAT'S THIS IMAGE?
IS THIS WHAT IT'S SEEING?

IT'S AFTER TENCHI NOW?

WASHU! INJECT ME!
HURRY !!

ARE YOU SURE?

JUST DO IT!
OR ELSE TENCHI...

ALL RIGHT.

DRAT... THAT THING POWERED UP BY TAKING RYOKO!
I CAN'T GET LIGHT HAWK WINGS... MUST NEED TIME TO RECHARGE!
UFF
HFF

SASAMI, RUN BACK TO THE HOUSE AND GET AYEKA'S GUARDIANS TO PROTECT YOURSELF WITH!
GOT IT?
WHAT?
B-BUT ... TENCHI !!

GO! NOW, SASAMI!
TENCHI !!
VSST

I HATE YOU...
I HATE YOU!
Squirsh

SPLOOOK
TENCHI !!
CAN'T MOVE MY ARMS... MY LEGS...
WH- WHAT?
!!
GLERSH
YOU... A LOT OF ENERGY...
TUMP!
SPLOOOOO

pa poom
UH...
SASAMI, RUN!
SPSSHK
I'LL EAT YOU UP!
DON'T TOUCH ME...
N... NO...
BLABLORSHT

OH ...
I KNOW, I KNOW! THAT WAS PRETTY SCARY...
...BUT IT'S ALL RIGHT NOW... OKAY? ♡
RYO ...
RYOKO ...

WAAAAAAAH!

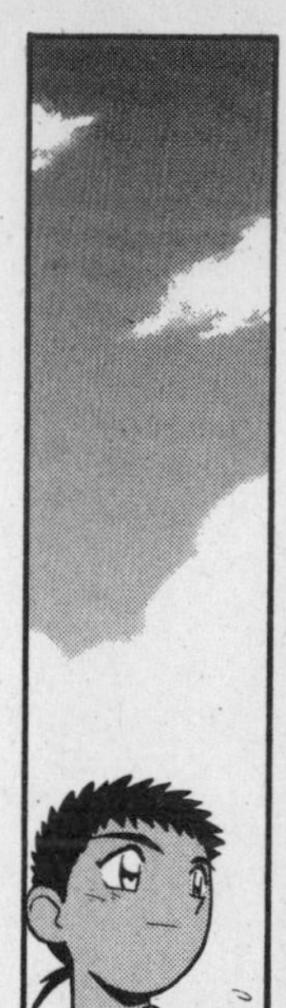

SO, UH, TENCHI?
WHAT IS IT, SASAMI?

WELL, IF...
...IF RYOKO HADN'T GOTTEN HER POWERS BACK, WHAT WOULD YOU HAVE DONE?
WELL, WE'D HAVE ALL BEEN TAKEN IN BY THE SHOU'OU...
NO, NO! BESIDES THAT...
WHAT WOULD YOU HAVE THOUGHT OF RYOKO... *WITHOUT* HER POWERS?

WELL...
I WAS AT A LOSS AT FIRST, BUT...

RYOKO IS RYOKO.
IT DOESN'T MATTER IF SHE HAS POWERS OR NOT.
YEAH! YOU'RE RIGHT! ♡
I KNEW YOU'D SAY THAT...
RYOKO! YOU CALL THIS AN IRONING JOB?
IT'S ALL WRINKLED!
GET OFF MY BACK! ONE OR TWO MISTAKES ... BIG DEAL!
IF IT WERE "ONE OR TWO," I WOULDN'T GET THIS MAD!
HA HA... TH-THEY SAY GOOD FRIENDS ALWAYS FIGHT...
YEAH.

Tales of Tenchi #4:
THE FERROUS CHEF

THIS IS GREAT! ♡
WOW. ♪

OKAY.
TENCHI, LET'S GET ON THAT ONE! ♡

HEY
YAK
YAK
PSST
WHAT'S WITH THAT CROWD?

HI, THERE. I'M SASAMI. ♡
TENCHI TOOK US TO THE AMUSEMENT PARK TODAY. ♡
WELCOME!!

OH! THEY'RE RECORDING A TV SHOW!
YOU KNOW ABOUT THIS SHOW, MIHOSHI?

FERROUS CHEF! IT'S GREAT! AMATEUR COOKS HUMILIATE THEMSELVES BY CHALLENGING THE ASSIGNED COOKING TOPIC!
SALT
IT SOUNDS LIKE A MEAN SHOW.
YES, IT IS.

SO WHAT'S TODAY'S THEME?
OHH! AHH!
LET'S SEE...
YAK
YAK

"MAN HAN CHUAN SHI"*...

RYOKO... SHE'S SUPER, ALL RIGHT.

A WHOLE ROAST COW...

hah! Hah! tah!

TODAY'S THEME: MAN HAN CHUAN SHI

*COOKING FOR THE CHINESE IMPERIAL COURT. SUPER DELUXE, SUPER LUXURY, SUPER VOLUME.

TENCHI, DID YOU SEE MY MAGNIFICENT COOKING? ♡
SURE...
BRUTE FORCE BARBECUE, HEAT PLUS COW...
WITHOUT EVEN SEASONING IT.

IT'S SO SAD...

YOUNG PEOPLE THESE DAYS JUST CAN'T COOK!
NO JOKE! WHEN WE ASSIGNED STUFFED CABBAGE ROLLS, ONE KID WRAPPED THE INGREDIENTS IN LETTUCE LEAVES.

OF COURSE, WITH TODAY'S ASSIGNMENT, NOT EVEN PRO CHEFS COULD EASILY...

Chp!chp!chp!

blubba
plip
plap!
blub
plup!

!
Szzzl!
Szzl!

ALL DONE ♡
TA-DAA!
WOW, SASAMI! YOU'RE THE GREATEST IN ALL OF JAPAN!
HEH HEH! AW, SURELY NOT!
SHE'S MY SISTER, AFTER ALL. ♡
WHA...
WHAT'S WITH THIS KID?
H-HEY, COME TRY IT!
DELICIOUS!
D...
SEE?

NO, NO, NO! ROOTS AND TUBERS START IN COLD WATER...
...AND LEAFY VEGETABLES START IN *HOT* WATER! ARE YOU *STUPID*?
WHAT A MEAN-SPIRITED ANNOUNCER!
CUT OFF THE POTATO SPROUTS. THEY'RE *POISON!*
POT CALLING THE KETTLE BLACK, RYOKO?
BET HE COULDN'T EVEN DO IT HIMSELF.
BRRRRNG

YOU GUYS HAVE A LOT OF NERVE!
WHAT DO YOU MEAN *BY* THAT?
A
W
JUST WHAT I SAID. ♡
W
HELLO, MASAKI RESIDENCE.
YES?

YOU CAN'T EVEN GUT A FISH.
YOU'RE ONE TO TALK!
YOU NEVER TIRE OF THIS, DO YOU?

WHAT?

SASAMI, ARE YOU ALL RIGHT?
poip!
OH...UM, SORRY I RAISED MY VOICE.
IT'S THE TV PEOPLE...
...THEY WANT ME ON THEIR SHOW!
TV?
TOOOT! TOOOT!

TENCHI WAS VERY WORRIED ABOUT ALL THE PUBLICITY, BUT HE FINALLY AGREED...AFTER MY EARNEST PLEADING.
THANKS, TENCHI. ♡
SO THAT'S HOW I WOUND UP IN A KIDS' COOKING CON-TEST!
WE HADN'T BEEN ON VACATION IN A WHILE... AND I WANTED TO GO TO TOKYO AT LEAST ONCE. ♡
TOKYO 1970 DOESN'T COUNT! -ED.
hic!
SASAMI. ♡
C'MON, HAVE A DRINK! ♪
LET'S CELEBRATE!
HEY!
RYOKO !!
STOP IT, RYOKO! SASAMI IS A MINOR!
YOU DRINK, THEN.
GRRR!
AYEKA !
HA, HA...
I FEEL UNEASY ABOUT THIS...
RYOKO, STOP IT ALREADY!
C'MON, TENCHI, YOU TOO! DRINK UP! ♡

URP...
I...I GUESS WE MADE IT SAFE AND SOUND...
SOMETIMES YOU CAN'T SAY NO TO RYOKO...
ARE YOU ALL RIGHT?
I'M FINE...
...I *THINK.*
PATHETIC. CAN'T EVEN HANDLE 20 OR 30 CANS OF BEER?
SHLURRP
I MISS THE *HUMAN* RYOKO.
WAIT! WHERE'S MIHOSHI?
OH, MIHOSHI? SHE'S *THERE...*
...GETTING A TASTE OF RELIGION, TOKYO-STYLE!
STOP HER!
THIS *ULTIMATE* CHARM WILL LEAD YOU TO PARADISE...AT A 90% DISCOUNT PRICE OF 50,000¥!
WOW! A 90% DISCOUNT?

HI-HI, SASAMI! THANKS FOR COMING SO FAR!
I'VE BEEN WAITING FOR YOU. ♡
AKAGAWA TV 11

OH, HI!
GOOD TO MEET YOU!
BLUSH
THE PLEASURE'S ALL MINE.

IT'S IN YOUR HANDS, WASHU.
NURSE'S OFFICE

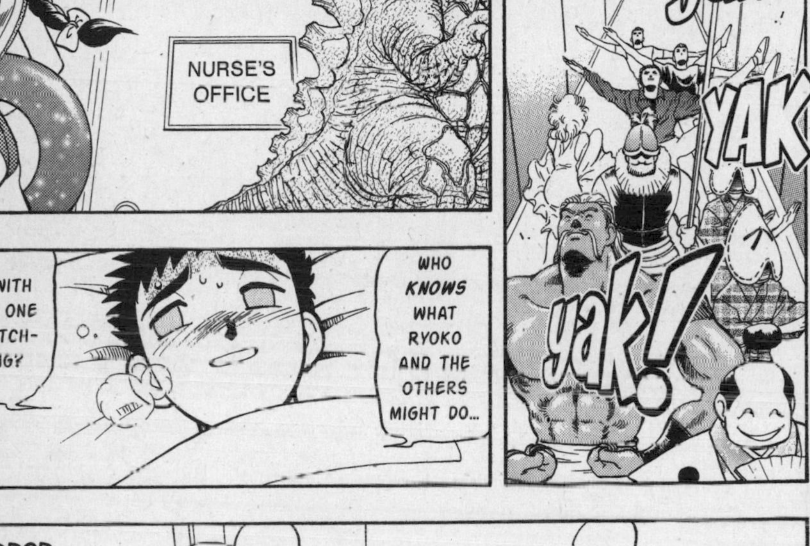
YAK yak!
YAK yak!
...WITH NO ONE WATCHING?
WHO KNOWS WHAT RYOKO AND THE OTHERS MIGHT DO...
DROP THE MALLET!
WELL...
I'LL TRY.
OKAY?
KAKRESSH
GGK!

ALTHOUGH SHE'D LIKE TO STAY BY TENCHI'S SIDE, AYEKA HAS TO ACCOMPANY SASAMI...
OH, LORD TENCHI! PLEASE BE SAFE...
THE FINAL MATCH WILL BE STAGED HERE TOMORROW.
THIS IS AMAZING! ♡
TEE HEE! OH, WHO KNOWS?
YOU'RE THE YOUNGEST CONTESTANT, BUT YOU'LL DO FINE! I'M SURE YOU'LL MAKE IT TO THE FINAL ROUND.
IT'S A THREE-PART COMPETITION. FIRST, THE DISHWASHING RACE. THEN AN INGREDIENTS KNOWLEDGE MATCH. THREE FINALISTS MOVE ON TO THE BIG COOKING CONTEST.

OH! THERE HE IS.
!
THAT'S THE *PREVIOUS* CHAMPION, KAGATO-KUN.
?! KAGATO ...KUN?
KAZUMA KAGATO (11 YEARS OLD)
THAT FACE! BAD KARMA...
IT COULDN'T BE
HI-HI THERE, KAGATO-KUN! YOU TWO SHOULD MEET!
THIS IS SASAMI, WHO CAME ALL THE WAY FROM OKAYAMA.
I GUESS SHE'S YOUR *RIVAL*.

PLEASE NOTE: THIS STORY HAS NOTHING TO DO WITH THE *REAL* KAGATO!

EEK!!
HA HA HA!
CHIEF... PLEASE!
OH HO?
SHE'S MY SON'S GREATEST RIVAL, EH?
SHIIK
LET'S JUST HOPE YOU DON'T GET *STAGE FRIGHT* AND MISTAKE *SALT* FOR *SUGAR!*
HA HA HA HA
GRRR

KAZUMA, SHOW THEM.

YES.

HEH HEH... ♫

AND *WE* SURE HOPE THAT *YOUR* BRAT DOESN'T MESS UP HIS LITTLE FINGERS WITH THOSE SHARP, SHARP *KNIVES!*

A- AYEKA!

CHOP! CHOP! CHOP! CHOP! CHOP!

HOW WAS *THAT?* STILL THINK HE MIGHT CUT HIS FINGERS?
ENOUGH.
OOOOH
WOWWW!!!

CHOP! CHOP! CHOP! CHOP!
...
W...

ALL RIGHT, SASAMI! SHOW HIM WHO'S BOSS!
GRRRRRRR
AYEKA, CALM DOWN!

OH... NOW I KNOW YOU.
YOU'RE THE LITTLE GIRL WHO MADE THE CHINESE FEAST ON THE FERROUS CHEF SHOW.

HMPH
I CAN'T WAIT FOR TOMOR-ROW.

EXCUSE ME.
CHIEF ...

I'VE NEVER SEEN ANYONE SO RUDE.
NOW, NOW!
SORRY ABOUT THAT. HE'S THE OWNER AND CHEF OF A FAMOUS RESTAURANT IN GINZA.
HE'S A MAN OF, UM...STRONG INDIVIDUALITY.

OUR FAMILIES ARE A LITTLE *WEIRD*, BUT LET'S DO OUR BEST TOMORROW!
I WON'T LOSE TO YOU.

HUH?

I WON'T LOSE TO YOU OR *ANYONE!* I *WON'T!*

PLEASE, YOUNG MASTER! WAIT!

FWSH!

I'M SORRY ABOUT THIS!

OH!

YOUNG MASTER!

TMP TMP

WHAT'S UP WITH THEM?

HMPH

THAT'S WHAT I'D LIKE TO KNOW!

IT REMINDS ME OF MY SPACE PIRATE DAYS...
A TV STATION IS SO FULL OF INTERESTING PEOPLE AND COSTUMES!
ON AIR
HEY! I KNOW THIS SHOW! ♡
The Friday Night Ghost Show
RECORDING
No Admittance
SO THEY RECORD IT HERE?
I'LL JUST TAKE A QUICK LOOK.
FSSSSHT
WHAT? AGAIN?
CUT!!!

I'M SORRY... JUST ONE MORE TAKE?
THE LIGHTING IS ALL WRONG!
GIMME A SPOT HERE!
I HATE WORKING WITH AMATEURS!
DEGENERATE IDOL STAR...GRIPING ABOUT HER DESIRES WHEN SHE CAN'T EVEN SEE HER OWN SUCKY ACTING!
DIRECTOR
SCENE 37, TAKE 4! ACTION!
ALL RIGHT...
"THE SCHOOL IS SCARY SO LATE AT NIGHT..."
"I'D BETTER GRAB MY NOTEBOOK AND RUN."
POIP
HUH?
WHERE AM I?
FWSSSHT

KAKAGAWA
TV 11

LORD TENCHI, ARE YOU ALL RIGHT?
YEAH, I'M FEELING MUCH BETTER NOW.
WHERE'S RYOKO?
SORRY TO KEEP YOU WAITING. ♡
SHE WAS POKING HER NOSE INTO THE FILMING OF "THE FRIDAY NIGHT GHOST SHOW."
BONK!-SKRK
OWW!!
WASHU! RYOKO!
"THE FRIDAY NIGHT GHOST SHOW!" OOOH!

GOING THROUGH WALLS, FLOATING IN THE AIR, GETTING DRUNK...SHE'S QUITE THE LITTLE TROUBLE-MAKER.
HOW COULD YOU?
IT WAS JUST A LITTLE PRANK!

I SAID I WAS SORRY!

LET'S GET BACK TO THE HOTEL FOR SOME DINNER.

YEAH. ♡

!

YOU WANT ME...

"DON'T WIN AGAINST HIM"...EH?

*THE "SECOND COOK" HAS THE MOST AUTHORITY IN A KITCHEN AFTER THE CHIEF COOK.

SO THE FATHER WANTS HIS SON TO TAKE OVER THE FAMILY BUSINESS SOMEDAY.
OHH, NICE AND WARM! ♡
BUT THE SON DOESN'T REALLY WANT TO BE A CHEF.
HE'S ARRANGED IT SO THAT HE CAN PUT HIS "RETIREMENT PLAN" INTO EFFECT... AFTER HE WINS THIS COMPETITION THREE TIMES IN A ROW!
YEAH...
I SAW YOU ON TV THE OTHER DAY. YOU WERE SPLENDID. YOU COULD BE THE ONE TO STOP KAZUMA'S WINNING STREAK.
I KNOW THIS IS A HOPELESS REQUEST...
...BUT THE BOY'S LIFE IS HIS OWN.
IT WOULD BE ALL RIGHT IF THIS WERE HIS AMBITION...BUT AT THIS RATE, HE'LL BE THE CHIEF'S PUPPET FOR THE REST OF HIS LIFE.

BLUB!

WHAT ARE YOU GOING TO DO?
WELL...

I CAN UNDERSTAND A *LITTLE* BIT THAT HE WANTS TO WIN...
...BUT IT WOULD FEEL BAD TO LOSE ON PURPOSE...
AND IT'S RUDE TO HIM, TOO.

WELL DONE, KIDDO!
SCRUB ADUB!
GLAH!

WELL, NO MATTER *WHAT* HAPPENS...
SHAAAAAAA

PITY NEVER DID ANYONE ANY GOOD!
SHAAAAAAAAA
YEAH...

NOT TO CHANGE THE SUBJECT...
SNKT
KIRIM

...BUT WHY DIDN'T YOU TALK TO AYEKA AND THE GANG?
JUICE?
YES, PLEASE!

WELL...
GULP...

...AYEKA DOESN'T *LIKE* KAZUMA'S FATHER, AND RYOKO WOULD...YOU KNOW...
HAHAHAHA
THAT'S TRUE! IF SHE TRIED TO SETTLE THE ISSUE BY *FORCE*, THINGS COULD *REALLY* GET OUT OF CONTROL!

HERE I COME THROUGH THE WALL JUST TO *TEASE* THEM A BIT, AND *THEY'RE* TALKING ABOUT ME LIKE I'M A *TERRORIST!*
I HEARD THAT!
IT WAS A GOOD IDEA NOT TO TELL HER!
hee hee hee

SHK SHK

...
...
THAT'S RIGHT...
PITY NEVER DID ANYONE ANY GOOD!
HMPH
THEY'VE GOT THEIR SCRUBBERS AND... THEY'RE OFF!
B
I'LL JUST TRY TO DO MY BEST!
TO BE CONTINUED!!!

Tales of Tenchi #5:
THE BLAME GAME

BRRBING
AND THE GRADE SCHOOL COOKING CHAMPIONSHIP HAS STARTED! FIRST UP IS THE "DISHWASHING RACE," A BRAND-NEW EVENT FOR US!
OUR COMMENTARY, AS YOU KNOW, IS BY MASTER CHEF HATTARI. SO, WHAT DO YOU THINK OF THIS MATCH?
THE ONE TO WATCH IS DEFINITELY THE CURRENT CHAMPION FOR TWO YEARS RUNNING, KAGATO KAZUMA.
WILL HE PULL OFF A *THIRD* WIN IN A ROW, A FEAT *UNEQUALED*? I THINK IT COULD HAPPEN!
OH, SASAMI ...GOOD LUCK!
HMPH. *WASHING DISHES*... SO... BASIC.
WE DIDN'T TRAIN HIM AS A *DISH BOY!*
GOOD LUCK, YOUNG MASTER!

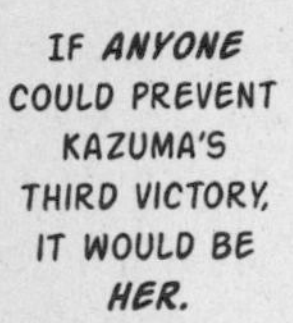
IF ANYONE COULD PREVENT KAZUMA'S THIRD VICTORY, IT WOULD BE HER.

OF COURSE, THE BRATTY GIRL HAS PROVEN HERSELF QUITE FORMIDABLE. I SAW THE TAPE...HER MAN HAN CHUAN SHI WAS A SPLENDID BUFFET.

OH, MY! SHE'S VERY FAST!
FWASH
fwish
IT'S NOT GOING WELL FOR OUR YOUNG COMPETITORS! LET'S CHECK IN ON THE CHINESE BUFFET GIRL, CONTESTANT MASAKI...
THE TECHNIQUE IS THAT OF AN AMATEUR, BUT SHE DOES MAKE IT UP IN SPEED!
THE FIVE WHO WASH THE MOST DISHES IN THIS 20-MINUTE EVENT WILL MOVE ON TO THE NEXT ROUND.
MOMMEEEE!
EWW! SLIMY AND ICKY!
shwee!

OF COURSE, IF SHE'S DOING TOO WELL...
...I MIGHT... INTERVENE!

I-I KNOW THIS IS A HOPELESS REQUEST...
...BUT PLEASE LET THE YOUNG MASTER WIN.

SASAMI...

WH-
WHAT'S
WRONG?
IS SHE
OKAY?
...
...

SKURRK

!!

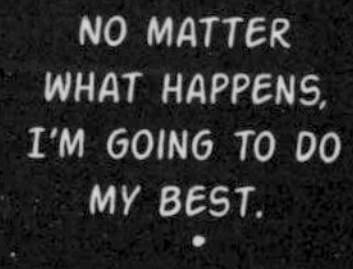
NO MATTER WHAT HAPPENS, I'M GOING TO DO MY BEST.
THAT'S WHAT I DECIDED...

...NO.
I CAN'T SLACK OFF HERE.

WHA...
WHAT SPEED!
I CAN EVEN SEE THE SOUND EFFECT!
fwish
fwash
fwish
fwash

SPLOOSH
I HAVE TO WIN!
HE'S A BLUR...
WOW!
BUT I CAN'T LOSE! I CAN'T!
FLP FLP FLP

DAD'S GOING TO KNOW HOW GREAT I REALLY AM!
TUP TUP TUP TWUP

SQUEAKY SQUEAKY!

A *SPLENDID* JOB BY KAGATO! WILL HE TAKE THE LEAD?
IT DOES LOOK THAT WAY.
BUT TIME IS RUNNING SHORT!
FIVE, FOUR, THREE, TWO, ONE...

BRRINNNG
TIME'S UP!
PHEW!
FOR A FIRST-TIME EVENT, THERE SURE WERE A LOT OF HIGHLIGHTS.
DID I WIN?
AND OUR FIVE SEMI-FINALISTS ARE...
KONNO HITOSHI, 87 PLATES. YOKOYAMA KAZUHIDO, 80 PLATES.
HEE
ASARI TASUKU, A WHOPPING 131 PLATES! AMAZING!
ALL RIGHT!
OOH! KAGATO WITH...197 PLATES? THAT'S EVEN MORE AMAZING!
BONK!
BUT WAIT! TH-THERE'S SOMEONE WHO HAS SURPASSED EVEN KAGATO-KUN!
COULD IT BE...
ONE OF OUR YOUNG CHEFS CLEANED ALL 202 PLATES!

MASAKI SASAMI-CHAN!

OOOOOOOOOOH

WOW!

YAY! YAY!

SHE DID IT! SASAMI, YOU'RE AMAZING!

HMM!
I'VE BEEN IN THIS INDUSTRY FOR 20 YEARS, AND THE WAY SHE WASHES... SHE'S NO AMATEUR!

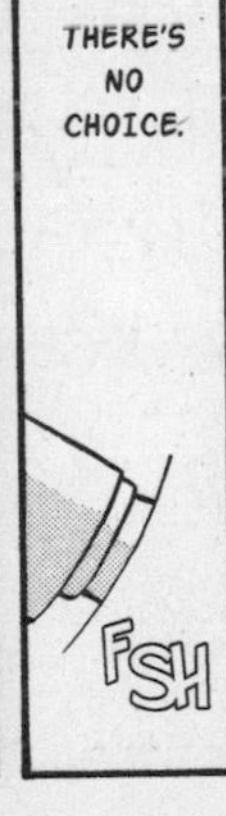
THERE'S NO CHOICE.
FSH

I HATE TO PLAN FOR KAZUMA'S LOSS...
...BUT BETTER TO CHEAT THAN TO LOSE!

WOULD THE FIVE SEMI-FINALISTS PLEASE FOLLOW THE STAGE HANDS...
FWM
PSH

OUR NEXT COMPETITION IS A COOKING QUIZ. GOOD LUCK, EVERYONE!
TMP
TMP

NICE WORK!
AIDE
OH...MR. KAGATO. YOUR SON IS SPLENDID.
THE MOMENT OF TRUTH IS YET TO COME.
SASAMI MASAKI

NO MATTER *WHAT* THE FINAL CONTEST'S COOKING THEME, THE INGREDIENT *SURE* TO BE USED IS...

THIS!

HE COULDN'T HAVE!
FINISH

GLAK!
SNAG
HEY, WASHU! THE SEMIFINALS HALL IS *THIS* WAY.

THAT'S NOT WHAT I WAS...
OH, I GET IT! I'M SORRY.

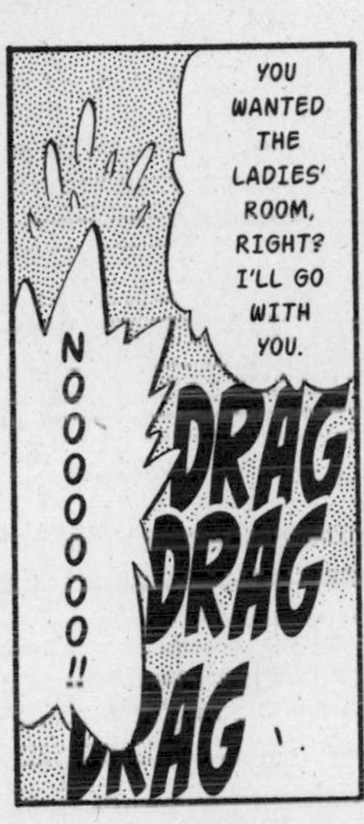
YOU WANTED THE LADIES' ROOM, RIGHT? I'LL GO WITH YOU.
NOOOOOOOO!!
DRAG DRAG DRAG

AND NOW THE FINAL QUES-TION!

FISH SAUCES HAVE BECOME POPULAR LATELY! NAM PLA OF THAILAND IS FAMOUS, BUT ONLY *ONE* OF THE THREE GREAT FISH SAUCES IN JAPAN CONTAINS *LIVE* MICROORGANISMS.
NAME *ALL* THREE FISH SAUCES *AND* THIS SPECIAL SAUCE!
220
230
VIVA WITH COOKING!

BZZZING
WHAM!
KAGATO-KUN WAS FIRST!
SHOTTSURU FROM AKITA PREFECTURE, ISHIRU FROM NOTO PENINSULA, AND DRIED FERMENTED MACKEREL JUICE FROM HACHIJO ISLAND...
...AND ONLY DRIED FERMENTED MACKEREL JUICE HAS LIVE MICRO-ORGANISMS!
DINGDING
SPLENDID! THAT'S EXACTLY RIGHT!
UNBE-LIEV-ABLE.
YEAH, I'M SURPRISED HE KNEW THAT, EVEN WITH HIS DAD'S RESTAURANT.
DINGDING
NO, I MEAN THAT GIRL... SASAMI.
HUH?
DINGDING
THE BOYS WHO REMAINED FOR THE FINALS ARE BOTH 11 YEARS OLD, BUT SHE'S 8.
DO YOU SEE?
THE CONTESTANTS LEFT FOR THE FINAL ROUND ARE ASARI-KUN AT 80 POINTS, MASAKI-SAN AT 230 POINTS, AND KAGATO-KUN AT 240 POINTS.
UH, UM...NOT REALLY.
THREE YEARS BETWEEN CHILDREN IS FAR MORE CRUCIAL THAN THE SAME AGE DIFFERENCE BETWEEN ADULTS.
I-I SEE...

EVEN SO, SHE COULD CARE LESS ABOUT SUCH A HANDICAP... HEH HEH HEH.

SASAMI...

...YOU'RE *MORE* THAN I EXPECTED!

AND NOW FOR THE FINAL ROUND!

WE'VE SPUN THE ***WHEEL OF COOKING FORTUNE***, AND THE THEME IS ***STIR-FRIED VEGETABLES!***

YOU HAVE TWO HOURS! **BEGIN!!**

FONDUE-STYLE SAUSAGE

COD POT AU FEU

BEEF STEW

STIR-FRIED VEGETABLES

MINCED RADISH AND CARROTS

SKRIP SKRIP
SKRIP
FWASH
HYAH!!

THEY'RE *BOTH* AMAZING.

MREOW!
POIP!

HMM?
SHWUSH

NO! IT CAN'T BE...

OR... COULD IT?

NO...

SUCH A SERIOUS EXPRES-SION...

!

HE DIDN'T CHEAT! HE WOULD NEVER!

IF I LOSE TO AN *8-YEAR-OLD GIRL*, MY CLASSMATES WILL LAUGH THEMSELVES SILLY!
ALL RIGHT! I'LL HAVE TO DO MY BEST, TOO!

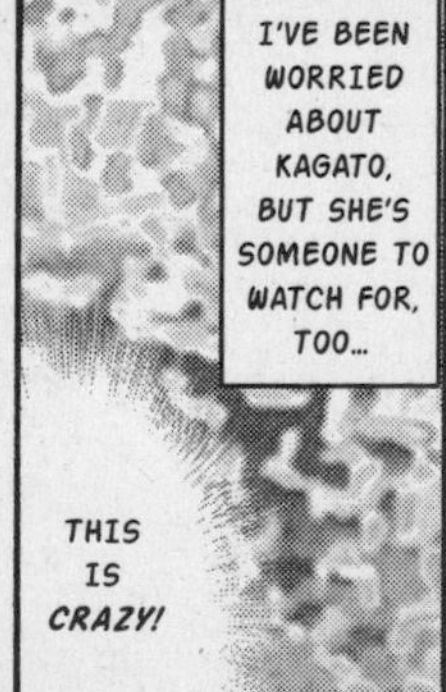

I'VE BEEN WORRIED ABOUT KAGATO, BUT SHE'S SOMEONE TO WATCH FOR, TOO...
THIS IS *CRAZY!*

...
WHEW!

SASAMI!
OH, NO!
SCRASH
YEEK!!
FWAK
OOPS!!
A HORRIBLE ACCIDENT! CONTESTANTS ASARI AND MASAKI HAVE BUMPED INTO EACH OTHER--AND THEY'VE FALLEN!
TOOM
ARE YOU ALL RIGHT?
I-I'M FINE. AT LEAST, I THINK SO.
!!
HEH! HER KNIFE BLADE'S BEEN CHIPPED!

LEAVE THIS TO ME AND GO DO YOUR JOB.
GRRRRR
OKAY, HURRY BACK TO YOUR WORK STATION.
IF YOU SAY SO!
OKAY.
ULP
DAMN HIM! HE DID IT ON PURPOSE, TOO...
MY KNIFE ...
M...
OH, NO!
RYOKO!

THAT FOOL! CAN'T HE LET IT BE?
CHIEF...
LIAR! I SAW YOU SMILE AFTER HER KNIFE GOT CHIPPED!
I DIDN'T DO IT ON PURPOSE! REALLY, I DIDN'T.
THAT WAS A MEAN TRICK! APOLOGIZE TO HER!
HUH?
PING!
OKAY, THAT'S IT! ♡
DON'T WORRY...I'M JUST GOING TO SHOW THEM THAT A LITTLE ACCIDENT ISN'T ENOUGH TO AFFECT THE MATCH.
RYOKO!!
HEY!

TINK

SHREEEEEEEEEEM

THERE... YOU SEE? ♡

WHAT'S *WITH* THAT WOMAN?

WAS THAT *MAGIC* ?

ALL RIGHT, YOU KIDS. BACK TO YOUR STATIONS.

GA!

RYOKO... ...THANKS.

BACK TO WORK! ♡

OKAY!

I'LL DO MY BEST!

FIGHT, FIGHT, FIGHT! ♡
CHOP!
TUP!
CHOP!
TUP!
I WONDER WHY...
...SHE LOOKS SO HAPPY...
BRRRING
TIME'S UP!
AND THE FINAL RE-SULTS...
!!
...
!!
THE WINNER IS MASAKI!
!!
...

MUMMA YAMMA
MUMMA YAMMA

HARD TO BELIEVE THEY'RE ONLY *GRADE SCHOOLERS.*
YEAH, REALLY ...
BUT THE BEST PART WAS THAT GIRL WHO WON!

YOU'RE NOT GOING TO SUCCEED ME IN MY BUSINESS? HOW DARE YOU...YOU FAILURE!
D-DAD!

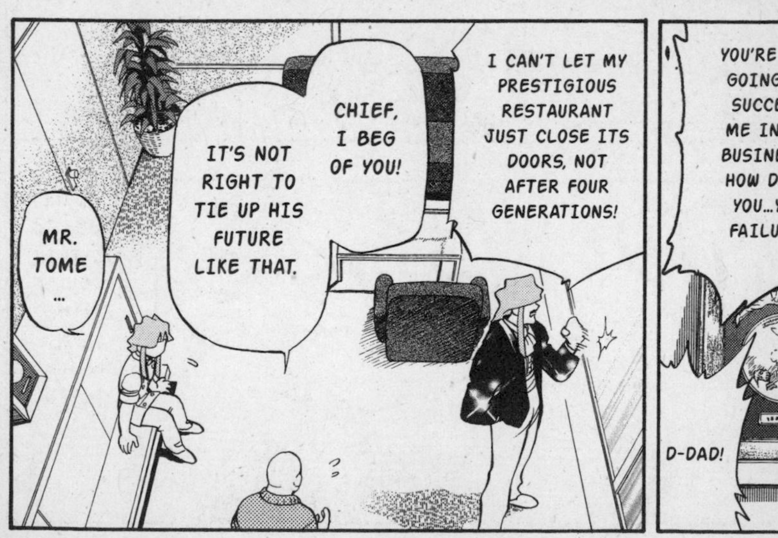

I CAN'T LET MY PRESTIGIOUS RESTAURANT JUST CLOSE ITS DOORS, NOT AFTER FOUR GENERATIONS!
CHIEF, I BEG OF YOU!
IT'S NOT RIGHT TO TIE UP HIS FUTURE LIKE THAT.
MR. TOME ...

DON'T BE AN IDIOT!
KAZUMA WILL TAKE OVER THE RESTAURANT! IT IS HIS LIFE PATH, JUST LIKE IT WAS MINE!

YOUNG MASTER!
!
!

WHY ARE YOU HERE?
HELLO! ♡

I REALLY HATE TO DO THIS KIND OF THING, BUT...
FWIP

BE CAREFUL, RYOKO.
THAT'S THE TROPHY CUP.
I KNOW.
WAIT!
HUFF PUFF

WHAT DO YOU THINK? NICE PICTURE, EH?
IT'S ONE OF THOSE SO-CALLED DECISIVE MOMENTS.
OF COURSE, IT'S A PICTURE THAT WASHU MADE IN PHOTOSHOP!

HMPH! THIS PICTURE PROVES NOTHING!
IT DOESN'T NEED TO. IT'S NOT FOR THE GAME-SHOW PEOPLE.
JUST...
HUH? WHEN DID YOU...

!
TH- THIS IS...

TOME, WAS IT? WOULD YOU MIND *TASTING* THIS?

IT'S OKAY...IT'S NOT POISON OR ANY-THING. ♡
POIP!

THAT'S RIGHT... THE DREADED MSG!
...

FORTUNATELY, SASAMI NOTICED AND DIDN'T USE IT.
IF SHE *HAD*, SHE MIGHT HAVE LOST. FOOD JUDGES HATE MIGRAINES!

JUST TELL ME ONE THING.
HOW DO YOU DO IT?
HOW CAN YOU COOK SO...SO *HAPPILY?*
WELL, IT'S BECAUSE I'M THINKING OF THE NICE PEOPLE WHO ARE GOING TO EAT IT, OF COURSE!
AND BECAUSE I LOVE COOKING ITSELF.
BUT, YOU KNOW...
TEE HEE
...*YOU* LOOKED HAPPY WHILE YOU WERE COOKING, *TOO.* ♡

I LOOKED ...HAPPY ?
WHO, ME?

mmmm

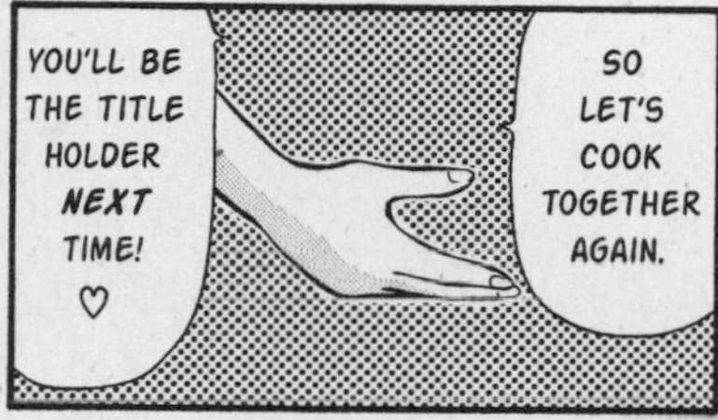
SO LET'S COOK TOGETHER AGAIN.
YOU'LL BE THE TITLE HOLDER NEXT TIME! ♡

heh

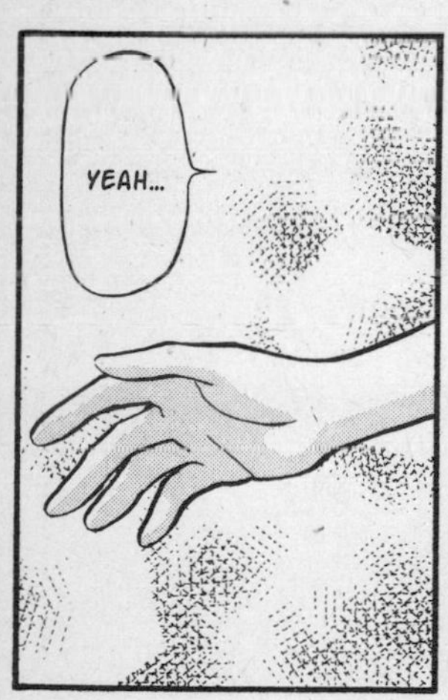
YEAH...

THERE'S NO STOPPING ME *NEXT* TIME!

CHILDREN *AREN'T* PUPPETS ON THEIR PARENTS' STRINGS...

VROOOM

VMMMMMMM
...

ahem

...
SAY, DAD...

HMM?
YES, WHAT IS IT?

DON'T YOU THINK THAT GIRL SASAMI WAS AMAZING?
I THOUGHT I WAS GOING TO WIN, AND IT WASN'T JUST CONCEIT...
I HADN'T GONE THROUGH YOUR RIGOROUS TRAINING FOR NOTHING.

SO, DAD...
...CAN WE STUDY HARDER, SO I CAN COMPETE AGAIN?

I TOLD HER *I'D* WIN NEXT TIME.

KA-ZUMA...

WELL SAID! THAT'S MY BOY INDEED! ***ALL RIGHT, TOME!***

HEAD TO THE RES-TAURANT! WE'LL START PRACTICING ***NOW!***

Y-YES, CHIEF!

VMMMM

WHHOOOOOOCHMCHMCHM

SASAMI! ♡ MIND IF I HAVE A SEAT?
OH, WASHU!
SURE. ♡

HAHA
I GUESS THEY BRING THEIR MAYHEM WITH THEM, HUH?
C'MON, TENCHI! HAVE A DRINK!
CUT IT OUT, RYOKO!
...
SASAMI...
HMM?
DID YOU CONSIDER *USING* THAT MSG CARROT...
...PRE-TENDING NOT TO NOTICE?
OH COME ON, WASHU.
YOU TOLD ME YESTER-DAY...
...THAT IF I GAVE IN TO PITY IT WOULD HURT US BOTH.
GOOD GIRL, SASAMI...
I JUST DID MY BEST.
tee hee

...YOU'RE A STRONG KID.
...BUT MORE THAN THAT...
YOU'RE A GREAT KID...
LATER...
HO HO HO HO HO HO HO HO !
VROOM
NOW WHAT'S GOING ON?
HO HO HO! WORLD'S GREATEST!
HO HO!
JUST YOU WAIT!
UM...THAT DIRECTOR CALLED BACK. HE WANTED RYOKO FOR A TV SPECIAL...
...CALLED "WORLD'S GREATEST HUMAN DISASTERS II"...

Tales of Tenchi #6:

SIMPLE JOYS

MY NAME IS *YOSHO*. MORE THAN 700 YEARS AGO, I CAME TO THIS WORLD FROM A DISTANT PLANET, *JURAI*. MY MISSION: APPREHEND *RYOKO*, THE INFAMOUS SPACE PIRATE.

AFTER AN INTENSE BATTLE, I WAS ABLE TO SEAL RYOKO AWAY...BUT MY SHIP, FUNAHO, WAS NO LONGER ABLE TO LEAVE EARTH.

HAVING LOST THE MEANS TO RETURN HOME...OR PERHAPS USING THAT AS AN EXCUSE...I MADE THE MOST OF MY LIFE HERE. I CHANGED MY NAME TO MASAKI KATSUHITO...AND 700 YEARS PASSED.
I KNEW THAT RYOKO HAD HER EYES SET ON MY GRANDSON, TENCHI. SENSING A CHANGE WITHIN HER, I ALLOWED THEIR ENCOUNTER.
AFTERWARDS, AS IF THE BREAKING OF RYOKO'S SEAL WAS A SIGNAL, WOMEN BEGAN TO FALL IN LOVE WITH TENCHI...GATHERING AT THE MASAKI HOUSE...
...AND BEGINNING A STORY ALL THEIR OWN.
SHHK
THE ROYAL TREE WHICH BEARS MY MOTHER'S NAME QUIETLY WATCHES OVER THEM...

...AS AUTUMN COMES ONCE AGAIN TO MY SECOND HOME...

OH!
MORNING, GRANDPA!
GOOD MORNING.

WHERE HAVE YOU BEEN THIS EARLY IN THE MORNING?
OH, YOU KNOW.
OFF TOWARD THE LAKE.
SHUP
SHUP

WHIP
WHIP
YOU'VE GOTTEN BETTER.
HEH HEH!
SHOO
TONK
HMM.
I TAKE THAT BACK!
YOU STILL HAVE FAR TO GO.
BONK!
OW!

GOOD MORNING, BROTHER YOSHO!
GOOD MORNING.
LORD TENCHI, HOW IS *YOUR* MORNING?
AYEKA, WHY ARE *YOU* HERE? IT'S *MY* TURN TO SWEEP THE YARD TODAY.
WELL, WE *KNOW* THAT BROTHER YOSHO ALWAYS EATS HIS MORNING MEAL ALONE...
...BUT SASAMI SUGGESTED THAT WE SHOULD HAVE BREAK-FAST *TOGETHER* SOMETIMES.
I SEE!
HMM... WELL, THEN.

heh

I GUESS I'LL BE INVITED, TOO?

OF COURSE!

MY HALF-SISTER *AYEKA*, WITH WHOM I SHARE A FATHER, HAS GROWN COMFORTABLE WITH HER LIFE HERE ON EARTH. BEING WITH TENCHI HAS TAUGHT HER *SIMPLER* WAYS...AND ALTHOUGH SHE IS THE FIRST PRINCESS OF THE JURAI ROYAL FAMILY, I FEEL SHE HAS BECOME *LIBERATED* FROM THE CONFINES OF THAT LIFE.

GRRM
GRRR
MINE! GIT YOUR PAWS OFF IT!
I HAD IT FIRST AND YOU KNOW IT!
GROWR
GRRRR

NOW, NOW. LET'S COMPROMISE, AND...
SHA
FWASH
FWISH

...I'LL JUST TAKE IT. ♡
WHAT?
♫

NICE WEATHER. ♡
YES, WHAT A CLEAR AUTUMN DAY.

JURAI AUTUMNS ARE NICE, BUT I LIKE AUTUMNS ON EARTH, TOO.
YES...

OH, *YEAH.*
HERE, THE MOUNTAINS TURN ALL RED AND PRETTY...NOT LIKE ON *MY* PLANET. ♡

MIHOSHI, DO YOU KNOW WHY THEY TURN RED?
HUH?

THERE WAS A BIG BATTLE HERE A LONG TIME AGO, AND THE BLOOD OF THE WARRIORS WHO DIED TURNS THE MOUNTAIN TREES RED IN AUTUMN.
YEEK!
HEY, HEY, *HEY!*

AHHHH...
IT IS A NICE PLANET... SO FULL OF ROMANTICISM.
NOT LOGICAL, BUT NICE ALL THE SAME. ♡

THAT'S SO TRUE. IN WINTER, WE WATCH THE SNOW FALL...
...IN SPRING THERE ARE THE CHERRY BLOSSOMS... AND COME FALL THERE'S...

MOONLIGHT SAKE AND SWEET DUMPLINGS.
WHAT'S THAT YUMMY MAPLE SOMETHING?
GRATED MAPLE! ♡
AUTUMN IS ALL ABOUT FOOD?
hmmmm
DID YOU COME TO EARTH TO EAT?

!!
aha!
?

WE COULD GO SEE THE MAPLES CHANGE COLOR!
LET'S DO IT! ♪

fwif
wiff

WIFF
WIFF

WHEW...
GRANDPA'S *LATE.*
IT'S PAST TIME FOR TODAY'S LESSON.

YO!

OFF TO TEACH TENCHI? HAVE A NICE ONE!
ah!
RYOKO...
!
WHAT WAS THAT SMIRK?
I DON'T LIKE IT!
SORRY.
IT'S JUST THAT...
...WELL, I'VE NOTICED THAT YOUR EXPRESSIONS HAVE GOTTEN KINDER...COMPARED TO HOW YOU WERE BEFORE...

gaaah!

D-DON'T BE CRAZY, YOSHO!
WE COULD SETTLE OUR BATTLE FROM 700 YEARS AGO RIGHT HERE AND NOW, YOU KNOW!

HEH HEH

HMPH!

FORGET IT.

THIS IS STUPID!

OH!

WEREN'T YOU HERE TO TELL ME SOMETHING?

THEY'RE READY FOR THE MAPLE VIEWING PARTY.

SASAMI ASKED ME TO TELL TENCHI.

I SEE...
I'M SORRY I TEASED YOU...
IT'S OKAY. YOU'RE TENCHI'S GRANDPA! I'LL LET IT SLIDE!
FSSSHT
SHE'S REALLY CHANGED.

RYOKO...EVEN YOU, WHO ONCE FOUGHT A *LIFE-OR-DEATH* BATTLE WITH ME, HAVE COME TO LOVE TENCHI...AND LOVE CHANGES *EVERYTHING*, DOESN'T IT?

I'M SURE THAT YOU WERE THE ONE *MOST* SURPRISED AT THAT! BUT THAT'S ALL RIGHT. IT'S *ALL* ALL RIGHT...

BOOOOM
CHAKKA
BOOM
BOOOOM
TA-DA!

WHEW! THAT WAS FUN. ♡
OH, *THIS?*
WASHU, WHAT IS THAT?

DOOM
WASHU'S SPECIAL KARAOKE JUDGING MACHINE, "THE ZAP-O-RAMA-VI"! ♡
BEEP BEEP, EEP!
Judging in progress

Brring!
51
IF YOUR SCORE IS LESS THAN *SIXTY*...
ZZZOT!!
ZZZAP
ZZZOT!!
!?
ZAP!

HOHOHOHO
I GUESS THAT'S AS GOOD AS IT GETS FOR A SONG BY AN EX-DEMON!
SZZT
SZZT
SZZT

PING
IT'S A LITTLE *EARLY*, BUT THE *STAR'S* READY TO GO ON... ♡

NOW SIT BACK AND LET MY BRILLIANCE TEACH YOU "THE SOUL OF SONG"!
47
POINTS
AYEKA!
STUPID MACHINE! STUPID MACHINE!
CRASH
HEY! FOR THE FIRST TIME, WE AGREE ON SOMETHING!
STOP IT!

LOOK, GRANDPA! THERE THEY ARE!
OH, TENCHI! ♡
SOB SOB! SOB SOB! SOB SOB SOB!
SORRY WE'RE A BIT LATE.
AW, WE WERE WAITING FOR YOU!
HEY, HEY!
WHAT ABOUT ME?
tink tink CLINK
SAKE
mmm
OW! HOT!
SHRRPP
GULP! yum
OH... THANK YOU.
HERE YOU GO, BROTHER. ♡
500ml
BEE
CHEW!

HAVE A DRINK, DAD.
SURE.
THE RED COLOR OF THE LEAVES MAKE YOU CONSCIOUS OF THE SEASON.
HMM... FRIED MAPLE LEAVES! A NICE TOUCH!

HMM! I NEVER THOUGHT ABOUT IT, BUT THE ***SACRED TREE*** DOESN'T TURN COLOR! HOW ODD.

EVEN IF IT ***HAS*** TAKEN ROOT ON EARTH, FUNAHO STILL HAS THE SPECIAL POWERS OF A ***ROYAL TREE.***

SO IT'S NOT ODD AT ALL.

...

OHHHH

FUNAHO...

SHAAAA
SHSHHH
WSSHH

YOU KNOW, FUNAHO...

I HOPE YOU DON'T RESENT ME FOR MAKING YOU TAKE ROOT HERE.
...I'M SORRY YOU HAD TO GO ALONG WITH MY SELFISH-NESS.

BUT I WANT YOU TO REALIZE *ONE* THING.

I *LOVE* THIS PLANET, THE PLACE WHERE MY *MOTHER* FUNAHO WAS BORN.

MY CHILDREN... THEY LAUGH AND PLAY HERE. I WANT TO LIVE WITH THIS LAND.

SKREE

KEEEE

VSSHHHH

SHEEEE

!

ZEEEEEEEEEENNNN

Shaaaaaaaaaa

FSSSH

A *VISION!*
FUNAHO...AWASH
IN *COLORED*
LIGIIT!

YOU'RE
LETTING ME
SEE THIS,
AREN'T
YOU?

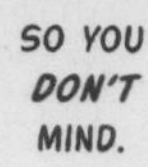

SO YOU *DON'T* MIND.
YOU LOVE THIS PLANET, *TOO*...

I AM A PART OF YOU...
...AND YOU OF ME.
THANK YOU...FUNAHO...

Tales of Tenchi #7:
PETTY ANOYANCES

RYOKO, COULD YOU CATCH RYO-CHAN?
GIVE IT UP.
MYEOW!!
THE PEEPING TOM (READ: DAD) ISN'T HERE THIS TIME, SO I CAN RELAX. ♡
HOW'S THE WATER ?
TENCHI-KUN IS TAKING IT EASY IN THE MEN'S BATH.

AUTUMN IS ENDING, AND AT LAST THE TREES ARE BARE. AS THE DAYS GROW COLDER, WE'VE DECIDED TO VISIT MY GREAT AUNT'S HOT SPRINGS.
OOH! ♡
THANKS!
OH, IT'S PERFEC
THAT'S GOOD.
I'D BEEN TOLD YOU HAD *TWO MORE* COMING. DID SOMEONE STAY HOME?
SHWEEEEEEEEEEEE
OH, I' SURE THEY'L
COME...
...HMM?

RMB RMB RMB RMB RMB
RMB RMB RMB RMB RMB RMB
WH-WH-WHAT THE...
ARE YOU ALL RIGHT?
WASHU, WHAT'S GOING ON?
IS ANYONE HURT?
AND WHERE'S EVERY-ONE ELSE?

WE'RE OKAY.
KOFF
TENCHI!
ISN'T THIS SHIP...
TENCHI, TIME TO PRAISE ME! ♡
GRAND-MA'S SAFE AND SOUND.
RYOKO!!
ALTHOUGH SHE HAS PASSED OUT FROM THE SHOCK.
THE HOT SPRING...THE HOT SPRING
SO THIS IS EARTH!
HEY! YOU'RE...

HMM?

WHOA! GRANDMA!

YUME!

WELL, WELL...IT'S WASHU'S DAUGHTER.

WHY THE HELL ARE *YOU* HERE?

I CAME ALL THIS WAY BECAUSE WASHU *TOLD* ME TO! "THERE'S AN INTERESTING EVENT--YOU SHOULD COME," SHE SAID. ♡

THAT'S SOME WAY TO SAY HI!

JUST KEEP IN MIND...
HOW COULD YOU?
NOW, NOW. DON'T BE SO UPTIGHT.
LADY WASHU! *SHE'S* THE VERY PERSON WHO CAUSED AN *UNPREC-EDENTED* CRISIS IN THIS GALAXY!

...YOU'LL HAVE TO BE ON YOUR BEST BEHAVIOR, YUME! ♡
?
THERE WE GO...
BEEP BOOP!
COULD YOU REMOVE THAT HEAD-BAND?
BEEP BOOP! BOOP! BEEP
WHAT IS IT?
ALL THOSE PESKY MEMORIES OF YUME'S ARRIVAL...
IF SHE WERE TO FIND OUT WHO WE ARE, I'M NOT SURE SHE'D TAKE IT TOO WELL...CONSIDERING HER AGE AND ALL.

COOL! YOU'VE GOT IT BACK TO NORMAL!
OF COURSE. WE UTILIZED THE 3D HOLOGRAPHIC MODEL YOU GAVE US...
SAFETY FIRST
THANKS FOR THE HARD WORK, EVERY-ONE!
THANK YOU.
THANK *YOU*, SASAMI.

BUT I GUESS WASHU DESERVES THE **MOST** CREDIT, FOR ACCURATELY MEMORIZING THE PRECISE LOOK AND FEEL OF THE HOT SPRINGS!
HAH HA HA
YOU MAY PRAISE ME MORE! ♪

SAKE
NOW THAT IT'S ALL FIXED...
BUT HOW WERE YOU ABLE TO PROCURE THIS MUCH ROCK AND HOT WATER?
A SIMPLE HYPER-SPACE LINK TO THE PLANET ABASON. YOU KNOW HOW SIMILAR THEIR MOLECULAR DISTRIBUTION IS TO EARTH'S.
...LET'S HOP BACK IN!!
HEY, RYOKO! NO FAIR JUMPING THE GUN!
GRRRRRRR
SAKE
KER
SPLOOOSH
FIRST IN! ♡
WHAT ?

WAIT, WAIT, WAIT!
YOU'RE GOING *IN*? IT'S UN-SANITARY! HEY!!
WHAT DO YOU MEAN, YUME? YOU'RE GOING IN, TOO. ♡
YOU'RE TELLING *ME*, THE FAMED GENIUS, TO TAKE SUCH UNSCIENTIFIC ACTIONS? WASHU, ARE YOU SERIOUS?
SURE I AM! IT'S THE CUSTOM ON THIS PLANET. ♡
THEY SAY, "WHEN IN ROME, DO AS THE ROMANS DO."
SHWIP
YOU...
WASHU!!
YOU HAVE A RATHER FLAT CHEST.
LEAVE ME ALONE!
I HAVE THIS BODY BECAUSE I LIKE IT.
BESIDES, WHO ARE YOU TO TALK?

HMM...THE UNIVERSE *IS* VAST. AND THERE *ARE* STRANGE CUSTOMS EVERYWHERE.
FINE! WE'LL JUST TAKE AN ACTIVE PART.
AS YOU WISH!

GREAT. BATHING WITH A MASTER CRIMINAL WHO PLOTTED TO CONQUER JURAI BECAUSE OF A DRINKING MATCH!
SHUT UP, ALREADY!
YOU'RE TURNING MY DRINK SOUR.
IT'S THE CUSTOM TO DISROBE, RIGHT?
OH, THERE YOU ARE...
!!
SO ISN'T THERE SOMETHING YOU HAVE TO DO BEFORE YOU ENTER?
YOU PERFORM A RITUAL TO CLEANSE THE BODY WITH WARM WATER, MASTER YUME.
E...
Y-E-E...
?
WHAT IS THE MATTER, JURAI PRINCESS?

BOOM!

YEEEEK!

SPLOOSH

HUH?

H...

SHEEEEOOO

Tok Tak Tak Tak Tok Tok

BLAH
AS A WOMAN, YOU SHOULD BE MORE MODEST AND...
BLAH
BLAH
YUME! WHAT KIND OF EDUCATION ARE YOU GIVING HISHIMA?

I DON'T UNDERSTAND IT!

YOUR WRINKLES SHOW WHEN YOU'RE ANGRY.

HEY! ARE YOU LISTENING?

BUT NOW I CAN DRINK IN PEACE, WITHOUT ANY DISAPPROVING LOOKS!

THE OLD LADY'S PRETTY DELICATE, IF SHE JUST FAINTS AWAY LIKE THAT.

I DON'T SEE MIHOSHI AROUND...

SHE'S LOOKING AFTER TENCHI'S GREAT AUNT.

SO YOU SEE...
...BY IMMERSING YOURSELF IN WARM WATER, YOU IMPROVE YOUR CIRCULATION *AND* GET CLEAN.
YOU CAN ADJUST YOUR CIRCULATION FAR BETTER WITH PHARMACEUTICALS, AND YOU CAN SANITIZE YOURSELF WITH CLEANSERS.

THAT KIND OF TECH HASN'T GONE MAIN-STREAM HERE.
AND, BESIDES...IT'S THE EARTH MENTALITY! LEARN TO ROUGH IT A LITTLE!

I SEE. THIS RESEMBLES THE BEHAVIOR THAT THE *DOUDOS* SHOW ON PLANET ABASON, WHERE THEY IMMERSE THEMSELVES IN NATURAL WARM WATER SPRINGS.
I'D CERTAINLY EXPECT SOMETHING MORE SOPHISTI-CATED--A MINIMAL AMOUNT OF TECHNOLOGY--ON EARTH...
HMPH! HOW PRIMI-TIVE!

HEY, RYOKO!
YOU'RE NOT SUPPOSED TO SWIM IN THE BATH!
FSSSSH
FOOL!
IT'S MORE *FUN* WHEN IT'S NOT ALLOWED! ♡

TIME FOR A DIVE!
YOU *MUSTN'T* BECOME STEEPED IN VICE!
I WISH I COULD DO THAT...
BLUB!
BLUB!

HIC... HUH?
WAS THERE SUCH A DEEP SPOT BEFORE?

!

WHAT'S *THAT?*
DANGER
DON'T PULL!!
DANGER
Don't touch!

ARE YOU TELLING ME THAT WASHU DOESN'T KNOW?
HOW RUDE!
OF COURSE I KNOW.
THE DOUDOS?
OF PLANET ABASON?
IT'S THE MAMMAL CONSIDERED TO BE THE MOST VICIOUS CARNIVORE IN THE UNIVERSE.
MYEEEEAAAAAAA
ITS MASSIVE FORM IS MORE THAN 10 FEET TALL, AND ITS CRY...
YES, SOME-THING JUST LIKE THAT...
SPLSH SPLSH SPLSH SPLSH

HUH?
MREEEEEEEAAAG!

HEY! WHY IS THERE A DOUDO HERE? WELL, YUME?
SOMETHING'S WRONG! WHAT HAPPENED?
!!
AAAAGG
MMREEE
WH- WHAT THE...
MASTER YUME!

FSSHZ
WHAT THE HELL IS THAT?
TH...
DANGER
HANDS OFF!
DON'T PULL
THAT PLUG!
WHO SAID YOU COULD PULL THAT OUT?
IF IT SAYS "DON'T PULL," YOU GENERALLY PULL!
PRIME SUSPECT
WHAT IS THAT PLUG?
IT OBSTRUCTS THE HYPER-SPACE LINK CONNECTING EARTH AND ABASON. THE RIFT HADN'T SEALED YET
AND SHE...
SOB
IS EVERY-ONE ALL RIGHT?
THAK
OH! LORD TENCHI! ♡
TENCHI... ♡
HISHIMA!!

FWSSH
HAH!
FWASH
HUH?
WOW, IT STOPPED THE BLADE WITH ITS BARE HANDS! ♡
NOW FACE ME!

YAAAA!!
WHAAM
URRK
HISHIMA!!
SKRR
RRSH
I'M BEING PUSHED BACK!
THIS CAN'T BE!

PWOP!
AAAACK!!

LORD TENCHI IS IN DANGER!
WHAT SHOULD WE DO?
PERHAPS IF YOU'D TAUGHT HER TO BE MORE LAW-ABIDING...
heh heh heh heh
A CHILD'S MISCONDUCT IS THE PARENT'S RESPONSIBIL-ITY, RIGHT?

SPSSSSSST
DON'T CHANGE THE SUB-JECT!

URK

OH, PLEASE!
YOU DON'T KNOW WHAT YOU'RE UP AGAINST!
ZREEE
EEEE
MASTER YUME!

MREE EEAA AU GHH!
RROWR
WHAT ARE THOSE MERRY SOUNDS...
HUH?
PAD PAD
...OVER AT THE BATHS?
MEE
EEK
HA! YOU'RE A LIFE FORM WITH NOTHING BUT BRUTE STRENGTH!
THERE'S NO WAY YOU COULD BREAK THOUGH MY *HYPERPRO-TONIC INVULNERABLE COSMIC STRING BARRIER!*

CHMP
CHMP
GACK! THAT'S SO UNSCIEN-TIFIC!
UH... UM...
HUH?
SKRAKK
NO! IT'S AN ENDANGERED SPECIES!
CHAK
DAMMIT! I'LL TAKE THIS ATOMIC BLASTER AND...
KYOOUM
HIS CHARAC-TER DESIGN IS SO EYE-CATCH-ING!
SIGH...
FWSSH
MASTER YUMEI LEAVE THIS TO US!
HISH-IMA!

LORD TENCHI! TRY TO DRIVE IT BACK WITHOUT HURTING IT!
ARE YOU NUTS? YOU'RE CONTRADICTING YOURSELF!
FWA
WAK
OH, MY!
I CAN'T BELIEVE IT!
THE LUXURIOUS FUR!
AND THE UNPRINCIPLED, SAVAGE BLOWS!
THE INDISCRIMINATE VIOLENCE!

FLUFFY!!
THERE'S NO DOUBT ABOUT IT...IT'S...
MRP?

AWW! IT *IS* FLUFFY ♡

RREOW!! ♡

M-MIHOSHI...
IS HE AN ACQUAINTANCE OF YOURS?
OH, YEAH! HE IS! ♡
I FOUND HIM CAUGHT IN A TRAP AND SAVED HIM, BACK WHEN I WAS WORKING ON THE PLANET ABASON.

THAT LOOKS LIKE A *CAT* TO YOU?
PRRRRRRRR
ISN'T HE A CUTIE WOOTIE? ♡

UNH...
WHY DOES MY HEAD FEEL SO HEAVY?
AND WHAT'S THIS RACKET?
KA DOOM

GREOW?

I CHALLENGE YOU TO A DUEL ONCE MORE!

SHEESH, GUESS WE HAVE TO START OVER.

HEY, WASHU!

WHY *NOT* REBUILD THIS PLACE INTO A HOT SPRING RESORT AND HYPER-TECHNOLOGY INDUSTRIAL TRAINING FACILITY?

TO BE CONTINUED!